S0-FQW-685

# Salt with the Sacrifice

# Salt with the Sacrifice

## Rebecca Crowder Clark

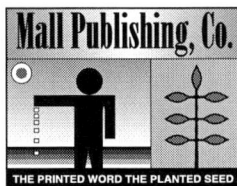

**Mall Publishing, Co.**

THE PRINTED WORD THE PLANTED SEED

HIGHLAND PARK, ILLINOIS

Copyright © 2004 Rebecca Crowder Clark

Printed in the United States of America

Published by:
**Mall Publishing**
641 Homewood Avenue
Highland Park, Illinois 60035
877.203.2453

Cover Design by Andrew Ostrowski

Book Design by Marlon B. Villadiego

All rights reserved.  No part of this book may be reproduced or transmitted in any form or by any means, graphic, electronic, or mechanical, including photocopying, recording, taping, or by any information storage or retrieval system,without the permission in writing from the publisher.

Unless otherwise noted, all scripture quotations are from the King James Version (KJV) of the Holy Bible.

**ISBN 0-9748686-7-1**

For licensing / copyright information, for additional copies or for use in specialized settings contact:

**Rebecca Crowder Clark**

*Mableton, GA  30126*
Email:  becmin@juno.com

# ACKNOWLEDGEMENT

God dictated this sermon/book to me during 1996-2000.  I want to thank Him for His patience at those times when I was too busy to listen.  He waited and spoke when I was quiet and attentive.

## Thank You To

*Gable, my husband, for allowing me to do whatever it takes to do the will of the Father. He insisted on waiting until the book was finished before knowing anything about its content.  Why?  Because he knows and trusts that I, a woman, can also hear from God.*

*Wyona B. Crowder, Howard Crowder (deceased), Beverly and DeWayne - my parents and siblings - for encouragement.*

*Garvin Byrd, my uncle, for revealing to me that writing this book was part of my salt.*

*Iris & Chris Adams for allowing me to preach this message at The Rock Christian Church 5 years ago where their members are still heard to say, when they do something extra, "Pastor, this is my salt."*
*Frances Crowder for always, always, always encouraging me and reminding me that life is what we make it.*

*Frances Garmon for not only surviving but succeeding!*
*The late Bishop Benny G. Isom for encouraging me to always go when God says go.*

*Eld. Joe Houston for teaching me to always praise God.*

*Eld. Johnny Lockart for teaching me "HOW to learn more about Christ. Oh, how THAT changed my life for the better.*

*Mins. Shawn and Janitris Cook who said "It's time".*

*Prof. William Chaney, Pastor at The Rock Christian Church and professor at Beulah Heights Bible College, for truly showing me Jesus.*

*Beulah Heights Bible College President Samuel Chand, the staff and students for teaching me to "Break the Mold and Bridge the Gap".*

# INTRODUCTION

Salt with the Sacrifice began as a sermon and still is one that just happens to be long enough to be a book. It was written for those who have been making a sacrifice to serve the Lord but that sacrifice has become routine or has caused complacency and maybe even arrogance. It explains how God still wants our sacrifices even in this dispensation of grace and wants them to be prepared with "salt".

# TABLE OF CONTENTS

# CHAPTER ONE

*I*n Leviticus 2:13 (KJV), God instructed His people to offer sacrifices to Him for the purging of sin. In His instructions, He included "and every oblation of thy meat offering shalt thou season with salt; neither shalt thou suffer the salt of the covenant of thy God to be lacking from thy meat offering: with all thine offerings, thou shalt offer salt." God wanted salt with all the offerings - no exceptions.

Although we live under grace, our goings and comings for the Lord are still classified as sacrifices. As explained in the book of Leviticus, we, as they were, are required to add salt with it. The Old Testament is not obsolete; it is being fulfilled in this New Testament dispensation in which we now live.

This book is a guide to lay people. It points out how the person sitting on the pew or operating in an auxiliary should add actions (salt) to what we are already doing, which will cause us to have a deeper understanding of how the sacrifice kills the fleshly nature. Adding salt will also enable God to elevate us spiritually, in His kingdom, and earthly, in the local church.

The sacrifice is that which we already have or can get (time, money, service, good manners, sympathy) and although we give it, we struggle to do so because our flesh does not want to give. Salt is that which we do not already have and cannot see how we can afford to give it. He wants the "do not want to" and the "do not know how I'm going to" to go with it. Along with the sacrifice we already give, He wants more time, attitude, inner man, money, patience, special love thing, deepest hurt and closely held emotion that we believe we cannot afford to give. He wants us to salt our sacrifice with those things that will cause us to be completely wide open and available to Him.

I had been adding salt with my sacrifice for several years before I realized it. I was just doing what I was told to do. I have been stretched past that which I or anyone else thought I could be stretched. I have been moved in ways that I thought would break me and that is exactly what happened. That is exactly what needed to happen because I have steadily and steadfastly moved up in God in an outer way that people can see and also in my inner man in such a way that is almost impossible to explain.

God insists that we get on the ship (our sacrifice) and He also requires that we step off and walk on the water with Him (our salt). Leviticus 2:13, "And every oblation of thy meat offering shalt thou season with salt; neither shalt thou suffer the salt of the covenant of thy God to be lacking from thy meat offering: with all thine offerings thou shalt offer salt." Salt is not only one of the most important substances mentioned in the Bible, but it is a necessity of life.

According to Nelson's Bible Dictionary, salt had a significant place in Hebrew worship. It was included in the grain (Leviticus 2:13), the burnt (Ezekiel 43:4), and the incense offerings (Exodus 30:35). Part of the temple offering included salt (Ezekiel 6:9). It was also used to ratify covenants (Numbers 18:19, II Chronicles 13:5). Newborn babies were rubbed with salt in the belief that it promised good health (Ezekiel 16:4). During times of war, the enemies' lands were sown with salt to render them barren (Judges 9:45). In Roman times salt was an important item of trade and was even used for money. Many soldiers received part of their salary in salt. Jesus described His disciples as the salt of the earth, urging them to imitate the usefulness of salt (Matthew 5:13, Colossians 4:6).

## Meal Offering

In the book of Leviticus, the Lord gave instructions for the offering of sacrifices. He gave these instructions to the Levites, members of the tribe of Levi, when the people were encamped at Mt. Sinai, following their deliverance from slavery in Egypt.

This offering is translated meat offering in some versions of the Bible, but since this offering was bloodless and meatless, it is more meaningfully rendered meal (NKJV) or cereal offering (RSV). Meal offerings were prepared and presented to God as a meal, symbolically presenting the best fruits of human living to God to be consumed or used as He desired (Hebrews 10:5-10).

"In the meal offering a person presented to God a vicar-
ious consecration of the perfect life and total property of
another (Christ). There is no ground in this offering for
human boasting as though the offered were received by God
on the grounds of his own human effort. Rather, the recog-
nition of the person's unworthiness is emphasized by the
fact that meal offerings must always be accompanied by a
whole burnt offering or a peace offering (Leviticus 2:1,
Numbers 15:1-6)." (Nelson's Bible Dictionary)

Leviticus 2:12 says that the meat offering should be **seasoned** with salt. On first examination of this, I thought it
appeared as if one was to gather their sacrifice and prepare
the salt in a separate bag to be plopped down on the altar or
handed to the priest separately. A second look revealed that
the sacrifice was to be "seasoned" with the salt. The salt
was to be in with, not a separate part of, the sacrifice.
Matthew 5:13 says we are to **be** the salt of the earth. We are
not supposed to "carry" the "salt" around in our hand, separate from us, to be distributed as needed. Because we are
the salt of the earth, we are the savor which should be auto-
matic with our presence.

Some Christians begin their walk in laziness. Yes, it
seems we have service more now than at any other time.
Salvation/being born again is "in" now. People are slain in
the spirit and gifts operating galore. Lazy saints want a
quick fix. We want to "be delivered" at the touch of a hand,
in a high, quick service. Sinners want to "just be in the
presence of the Lord" and be slain in the spirit in hopes that
they will be magically delivered and stay delivered from

their sins without need of confession or denying the flesh. "Fix the circumstances of what I did Lord, but leave what I do alone. I want to continue to do the same bad things, but I want you to make sure there are no bad consequences. That's all I want, Lord." Some do not want to labor for the Lord physically, emotionally or spiritually by reading the Bible, praying and denying ourselves on a regular basis. We seem to have become more knowledgeable, yet weaker spiritually (II Timothy 3:5).

We seem to know more than previous generations about Him and what is capable of happening when we "get in His presence". We want Him to "fall" on or in us and wait to be knocked out in the spirit. He will do that. It is not a trick. But once He has done it, we have to get up and walk in what He did for us while we were on the floor. We may even work (as in wrestling with our flesh to deny the lusts thereof) in order to receive Him, but we may still want to sit down and expect <u>Him</u> to spend the rest of our lives taking away our problems. We wait around for the glory and anointing to come and take away all our problems. We ignore the beginning of the worship service, where our answer may be in the praise and worship songs or the sermon, because we are waiting for the altar call so we can get a quick fix. Sometimes we do not get anything in the altar call because God gave the answer in the sermon but we were not listening. We want to go to the altar so someone else will do the work. Because of this attitude, some of the same people keep getting "delivered" over and over again because they skip the instructions and head straight for the altar.

Do not get me wrong. I believe in blessings at the altar. The altar is good, but once we leave it, we need to follow the instructions given out during the singing and preaching to keep our deliverance.

God does give miraculous deliverances. Yet, some issues of life can only end by following a particular instruction such as is demonstrated in II Kings 5 with Namaan and John 9:6-7 with the blind man. Other issues of life will end only by living some instructions on how to handle oneself on a day-to-day basis after we leave the altar.

Have you read Proverbs lately? Deliverances remain only by knowing and living the precepts and principles of God's word. If we are delivered of the anguish of overdue bills one Sunday and the following week we spend our money on luxuries instead of the utilities, then anguish will return. In order to keep peace and deliverance, we must keep our minds stayed on Jesus. Who is Jesus? According to John 1:1,14, JESUS IS THE WORD. HOW CAN WE KEEP OUR MIND STAYED ON JESUS IF WE DO NOT KNOW THE WORD THAT IS HE? WE HEAR His word through preachers, teachers and our own bible reading. We can keep our mind stayed on our husband, wife or children all day because we know them, hear what they say and have a relationship with them. Our mind automatically wanders to thoughts of them. Does our mind automatically wander to thoughts of a stranger? No, because we do not know or have a relationship with them. Therefore, if we do not have a relationship with Jesus, how can we keep our mind stayed on Him? Relationship comes by spending time with Him, talking to Him, listening to Him, eating with Him. Isaiah

26:3 says "Thou wilt keep him in perfect peace, whose mind is stayed on Thee:…" It means rehearsing in our mind His words of life. How can we know the Word, if we do not hear it? Once deliverance comes at the altar, it remains for those who live by the words of Isaiah. I am sure that as we study the word of God more, we will need less altar time.

Another crucial part of Isaiah 26:3 is "…because he trusteth in Thee:". Our mind must be stayed on Jesus in trust! Keeping our mind stayed on Him does not mean constantly praying that we make it back to church on Sunday so we can get to the altar for another "fix". It does not mean constantly whining about our complaints as in "Lord, I wish You would..." or "do You think You can..." Some people continue living the same mess over and over again and every Sunday they are back at the altar for more "deliverance".

Leaders, do you get tired of "delivering" the same people with the same problems over and over again? Some may never grow in God unless you encourage them to see that it takes more than the laying on of hands and the falling out in the spirit. Some of "the called" will never get to a point where they can face the audience at altar call to help you pray for deliverance for others because they are still in the prayer line themselves. By all means, we should get what we need but also want a level of maturity that does not involve the need to get into the prayer line every Sunday. Pastors, do not like it that way just so you can continue to be glorified for being that preacher that makes people fall out and whose members cannot live without him? That will get laborious after a while.

This message is not for those who have occasionally been deterred from service because of illness, required work, a sickly child, an elderly relative that cannot be left alone or any such like. Committed saints, although deterred at times, always return to their position of dedication as soon as life returns to normal. They have those leaves that never wither. I believe that if this message does not apply to you then it should not offend you. Yet, on the other hand, have you ever heard that saying "A hit dog will holler"?

This message is written for those who always seem to have an excuse for not being able to participate, especially outside the church. (Most people will sit in the pews rather than go out into the hedges and highways. Well, if you are going to stay inside, you might as well be doing something while you are in there.)

There are those who have always been somewhat lazy about their walk with God. You know who you are. First, you were in high school and involved in extracurricular activities. Then, you were in college and had to study. Then you were married and had to take care of the house. Then you had children and had to get them to bed early because they had to go to school or because you wanted to get them out of your way. Then you got all the children out of the house and you still have excuses. You fail to realize that all those people who showed up for service and worked on an auxiliary had the same responsibilities that you did, yet, they managed to forsake not to assemble themselves together and to show their faith by their works.

Many of us at one time or another beat ourselves up because we do not do all that God asks us. There are some who, on average, know that we press our way to serve God. Are you always whining  about how you just cannot seem to do what God asks you to do, even though you know you can find that time?  Are you ever able to smile on a long-term basis because you know you are striving to serve Him in some capacity in your local church?  Do you work on service days just to get out of going to church?  Do you have the same problems and demands on Sunday morning that you have on weekday mornings, but on Sunday you just cannot seem to get out of the house on time like you do during the week? Do you refuse every request to do something concerning the church because you do not have the time, yet find yourself bored with nothing to do at the exact time the church activity you refused to participate in is carried out? You are lazy or fearful, which amounts to being selfish.

There are some who are well pleasing in God's sight and after His own heart.  There are some who have more responsibilities than you do, but they still manage to attend and participate in the worship services.  What makes you think you have the right to be more stressed out than the rest of us over the same problems?  So, you cannot say that no one can please God and that you are the norm.  Normal is not necessarily right.  Since you think normal is okay, then do not ask for special treatment in the judgment line when all the other "normal" people are being sent to hell for damnation.  Democracy does not rule in the Kingdom of God.  So, if it is possible to succeed, then it is also possible to fail.  We all know who we are.  Identify yourself.

You go to church when you feel like it.  You do not go when you do not feel like it.  You never go when you do not feel like it. When you go, you arrive when the "best part" is going on and disregard parts of the service that do not directly involve you. You do not want to be bothered with those services that are not on Sunday, maybe because there are not enough people present to see what you have on. You just want to sit back and observe.

Have you ever met those kinds of people who believe the only services the Lord really moves in are the ones when they sing a song or preach or read the announcements or testify? They complain about all the services except the ones in which they did something. Can you identify with any of the above scenarios?

# CHAPTER TWO

*A Sacrifice*

"And He cometh unto the disciples, and findeth them asleep, and saith unto Peter, what, could ye not watch with Me one hour? Watch and pray, that ye enter not into temptation: the spirit indeed is willing, but the flesh is weak" (Mark 14:38).

Attending church service is a sacrifice, even for those who are compelled to be there every time the doors are opened. The physical going is a sacrifice and always has been. Do you think people in the Old Testament wrestled with the **inconvenience** of making sacrifices? Our parents and grandparents fought poverty, lack of transportation and clothing to make their way to a place of worship. Today, we fight long hours at work, both parents working, single parents working and running the house alone, the media and electronics giving us all kinds of other things to keep our interest and instant gratification. Again, the attitude is "give me a laying on of hands, falling out in the spirit, instant deliverance NOW, so I can go do what I want to do" attitude.

We do not even want to witness anymore. We just want to invite people to church and send them to the altar for the preacher to lay them out in the spirit and get "the anointing" without lifting a finger to witness to or tarry over them.

Going IS a sacrifice. There is a scripture that says they were healed as they went. Apparently they were expected to start out going in their illness (Luke 17:14). What kind of illnesses do we have today? Are they physical, emotional, or financial? If not going and not participating has not brought about healing, why not try going and participating? Once the decision is made to sacrifice, also realize that God wants SOME SALT WITH IT.

The sacrifice is going because the spirit is indeed willing but the flesh is weak. The salt is the extra things we do that makes us realize the worth. For example, potatoes **are** potatoes, but potatoes with salt are much tastier. The salt on the potatoes cannot be seen, but it can be tasted and we know it is there. Potatoes without salt are very bland and will be left on the plate. When properly salted, they are eaten, enjoyed, digested, and bring nourishment to the body. Are you salting the earth, i.e., making yourself tastier and fit to be "eaten" so you can nourish/edify someone's life? The scriptures say we are the salt of the earth and if the salt loses its flavor, the earth will have no way to be salted. We will be treated like unsalted potatoes – ignored and left on the plate.

So what is our salt?  It should involve getting to church often (if we do not already), on time (if presently we are always late) and doing something after we get there (if we are presently a pew potato)!  Salt is acting like we want to be there.  Salt is acting like we realize that God has really been good to us.  Salt is acting like we realize we are not God, but God is God.  Salt is being lively  stones (I Peter 2:5).  Salt is repentance (turning aside from our way of doing things, such as going to service when we want to or skipping it completely, and turning to God's way of doing things which is noted in Psalms 7:17 as being righteous.)  What happens when He asks us to service and we say we have something else "better" to do?  Did I hear you say it is really not something better to do, it is just something **else** you want to do?   If you chose to do it over something else then aren't you saying it is better?

Let's be honest.  If we think going to service is better then we would go.  We do other things, not related to illness or work, because we think it is better.  Yes, that is the bottom line.  We think it is better or we believe it is more needful.  We do other things we <u>need</u> to do like grocery shopping, phone calls and visiting the hairdresser or the barber.  Let's decide to <u>need</u> to worship God and forsake not the assembling of ourselves together.  Let's need to enter into His courts with praise.  If He thought we would be **better** entertained doing other things **first**, He would not have said "seek ye **first** the kingdom of God and His righteousness..."

Do not start whining about wanting to do other things and have fun. He said seek ye **first**, not seek ye **only.**   He knew we would have other interest.  Seeking Him first helps us better choose those other interests, and keeps us out of years worth of the messes we can get ourselves into.

When we make excuses, we are saying other activities are better than God's activities. Now, I am not suggesting that we be in the church 24/7. I am referring to regularly scheduled services. The same services every week of the year. The services our schedule should revolve around instead of the other way around which is the way some of us have it now. Face it. If you do not plan to go outside the four walls, into the hedges and highways, at least do something concerning the inside of those four walls. It is amazing how Christians say "Lord, Lord, please come into my life but I really do not have time to be bothered with You just now." It is how some people do in their relationships. "Be my friend/spouse/church officer, only when I need you to be a trophy on my arm to make me look good, otherwise, do not bother me."

Before we gave our life to Christ, we decided other things were better than regular church services. When we repented, we decided to stop doing things our way and start doing things God's way. But some are still making the decisions as before about attending and serving during the church service. Is that repentance? No. Our thoughts are supposed to be different about church attendance and participation, not the same as or worse than before we were drawn to Christ. When we are a new creature in Christ Jesus, old things, like considering church service as a nuisance, are supposed to have passed away and behold all things become new, like we know we need church service now. If the service is not worth going to (and we know this can be true at times) then check yourself first. If you do not put anything in you do not get anything out.Second, ask God if you can go somewhere else. Third, intercede for whoever it is that is vexing the service. It can happen. All leaders are not concerned with leading the sheep to Christ. They are concerned about leading us somewhere, but not to Christ.

If we think we are saved and still do not want to be bothered by Christ, then something is wrong! How dare we ask God to come in to our life, and then tell Him we do not have time for Him or His works? We want a tee-shirt even though we did not run in the race. It ain't happening! If it upsets you that I ran in the race and got a tee shirt and you do not run in the race and do not get a tee shirt, then you are the problem. Old things, like wanting something for nothing, are supposed to be passed away. Consider the wedding. Both you and I were bid to come. I came and dressed in proper attire. You had other things to do and actually wanted them to change the wedding date and time to fit your schedule. What does the scripture say happened to those who were bid but did not come? Read Matthew 22. There are consequences for not participating. There are rewards for participating. Work. Reward. No work. No reward. There is a reward for denying self and making a sacrifice.

Flesh and blood will not enter the kingdom of heaven! When we insist on doing things our way (flesh), we will not get in because we will not be holy. When we move this flesh out of the way by attending service (sacrifice) and do something after we get there (salt), then we are more open to receive and we actually hear the preacher say something that applies to our situation and we actually get delivered! No flesh (go to church whether you feel like it or not) = blessings (you actually get something out of it and get some problems solved because you were there to hear!)

Read Luke 14. None of us are so special that any one can say "He did not mean me when He wrote the Bible." You may think that everyone else except you has to do it that way, but not you because you are special. You are special. So special that He is not going to change the book just for you. We go everywhere else, but we will not go to church. Example excuses: Rain, bad brakes, a bad cold that you do not want to give to everybody. You go to work in the rain. You drive all over town with bad brakes. You take your cold to work and give it to everybody there. More excuses: people mistreat me, my feet hurt, I have a headache. Yet, you still go to the hairdresser, the barbershop, the mall, the grocery store or to visit friends. You still go to the doctor and wait longer than you sit in church sometimes. You still go to restaurants. Come service time, you have excuses to stay home.

We all have problems. Some say "You do not know what I go through to get here." What you go through to get there is the salt, honey. THAT'S THE SALT!!! You are getting it right but think it is wrong because it does not feel good. That "what I go through" is the salt we are supposed to bring with the sacrifice! It hurts, so we think something must be wrong when it is actually just right. Instead of rejoicing, we say "It is not worth me giving it up. Nobody sees what I go through, so why bother?" No doubt, people in the Old Testament said the same thing. But, God sees how precious our salt is. That is why He requires it. We do not have a choice. He sees what we go through just to make the sacrifice. He sees what effort it will take for us to find salt. "For God is not unrighteous to forget your work and labour of love, which ye have shewd toward His name, in that ye have ministered to the saints, and do minister"(Hebrews 6:10).

Do not worry if others do not see what you must go through to sacrifice and season it with salt. It is not for others to see the actual salt. We only benefit from the results of you being seasoned with it. You taste better to us thereby edifying our lives which is your job according to Ephesians 4. We cannot reward you, but God can and will.

How many times have you stayed home from church with a problem and at the end of service, the problem was still there? You should have gone to church because staying home did not fix it. The Bible tells us to be the salt of the earth and every offering must be accompanied by salt. The things we do and the service we render because of Christ is deemed a sacrifice because "the spirit is indeed willing, but the **flesh** is weak." Yet, in all our required sacrifices, God wants some salt to go with those sacrifices.

In Leviticus, the salt was already supposed to be on the offering. Your salt is not supposed to be visible, yet it should be noticeable upon "tasting". What do you taste like? There was more to these offerings than just plunking down a pack of salt beside the offering. I know what you are thinking concerning the meat offering. Your first thought was salt being sprinkled on the meat. Your second thought was the salt had to go on before it was presented to the priests, but the offerings were taken to the priest live. Your third thought was how do you sprinkle salt on a live animal? Remember, the meat offering had nothing to do with animal meat. The offering was called meat in the sense of the substance of a thing or the good part of a thing. It consisted of fine flour and oil and frankincense. He did not want the salt put in a bag or box and brought along with it. He wanted the offering seasoned with salt. When do we season? Sometimes before, during or after preparation. Sometimes all three. God did not ask for a certain amount of salt from anyone because He knew all could not equally afford a certain amount. Sacrifices, tithes and obedience have always had specific requirements. Salt, offerings and works have pretty much been left up to us on how much to give – but in all three categories He has expected and expects something to be given. No one who is able to sacrifice can say they have no salt to give. We all have salt to give.

Example: You are married with three children and think you cannot be involved in anything other than attending services. Salt yourself by getting involved in the choir or the usherboard. Take the children with you and sign them up for the same stuff you are doing. Many choirs and usherboards allow the youth to participate with the adults. They have no age limit. All they require is dedication and commitment. You will all be at choir practice together so you will not need a babysitter at practice or during the service. Other people do it. If the leader says no, speak up for your child. Dare a leader who preaches "family, family, family" deny your request to have your children (well-behaved because you have taught them to be!!!) in your presence and serving with you in the church. (If your kids are too young, surely, there will be a teen in attendance with his/her parent that will babysit all the kids there for fun and for free.) Face it, you can find time to do everything else with the children in tow or dumped at someone else's house. When it comes to church, you want to use them as an excuse not to go. Am I talking to you? If not, move on. If so, be honest about it.

NOTE: Youth, find out God's plan for you before you run off creating your own plans. Many adults have created their own ideas of what their life should be like. Then when God speaks to them about His plans for their life, they had already amassed so many degrees, spouses, children or bills that they were unable to obey His will. Remember, seek ye first ...you know the rest.

The first person we drop is God. We work hard all day long and tired as a mule, we run three errands then we are too tired to go to Bible study. Whenever possible, we should put off one or two of those errands so we can be rested enough to go to Bible study. The act of putting off running some errands can be considered your salt. Run errands on your lunch break (salt) so you can go home right after work and prepare for Bible study. Even in a home business, set hours, unless an emergency arises. Everyone has to work overtime sometime, but not all the time. Sometimes, we run ourselves crazy during the week because our ego will not let us say "no" then on service or meeting days we decide we need to rest.

Why do we decide we need rest at Bible study, Sunday evening worship and revival time? Why get indignant because God expects us to go to church? I have had to turn down jobs and positions that would interfere with me going to church during particular seasons in my life when that was required by God. We usually do not get indignant when asked to work overtime for more money or run spending errands. "I do not care. I'm tired. I'm not going to rush to get to church." We are the ones who presented ourselves to the congregation and to the Lord and said we would go, do and be a part of the fellowship. We are the ones who will rush home from work or even take half a day off to run downtown to see some big name person speak about God or catch a one-day sale.

Two possible, practical reasons why going to church is a sacrifice: 1) It is our nature to want to do things our way. Again, Adam and Eve decided to do things their way when they tasted of the fruit. If we attend a bible believing church, we are taught how and why we should do things God's way. Serving God reminds us of our inability to help ourselves and we hate that; 2) We spend all our lives learning to be independent, and then we go to church and are taught that it is Gods' will that we let go of our independence and become totally dependent on Jesus. From birth throughout most of our lives, society dictates that we become independent. It starts with learning to hold our baby bottle and ends with getting a job and keeping it until retirement age and paying who we owe what we owe them.

It is definitely a sacrifice to serve God in the capacity of working in and around the church. We push, push, push to go to the grocery store after work. We push, push, push, to go to a play, concert or movie after Sunday worship, but we do not want to push, push, push to go to 6pm service or Bible study. Why? Because we are spiritually lazy! That's why Paul had to admonish us to be a **living sacrifice.** Everybody wants to die for Christ, but nobody wants to live (do things) for Him. We tend to push, push, push to do those things that please us, but when it comes to pleasing God, we do not have that mind to push, push, push (Ezekiel 3:4-11). He is the first person we cut out of our lives when things go wrong or when we are "tired".

This lesson is a simple one. It is about average people going to church doing something for God in His services. If no other place to serve God why not serve Him in the church building. Yeah, I hear you. The Bible said to go out into the hedges and highway. But, most are not doing that either! Inside the church walls need to be in order also to make the worship services conducive to receiving those who have been compelled to come into the sanctuary where we are to offer our salted sacrifice. Why compel people to come out of the hedges and highways and have no organized place of worship and teaching to send them to? It is pitiful when an evangelist gets a new convert and when that convert arrives at a place of worship to continue learning, the congregation acts like they could care less about him or themselves.

In the Bible, it could not have been pleasant to give up the best animal, fowl or first fruit of labor. It seems to have been a tedious job to make sure the best was chosen. In the case of animal sacrifices, perhaps every time another one was born, the owner had to inspect it to see if it was better than the last best one set aside for the sacrifice. Perhaps, every time another fruit was picked or a grain came to harvest, they had to check all the fruit and grain crops to make sure they chose the best of the best. Then they had to be ready at the time of the sacrifice and pack up the family to travel to the sacrificial area. Worse yet, sometimes the head of the family took the sacrifice, which left the mother and or children alone until he returned. After arriving at the place of sacrifice one had to stand in line waiting for the priests to inspect what was brought to be sacrificed. I wonder if the priest ever told anyone that their presentation was not good enough and sent them back home or to the market and then to the back of the line to start all over again? In the case of meat offerings, to make sure that the presenter did not have anything to brag about, the Lord required that it be offered along with a whole burnt offering or a peace offering which were made to atone for man's sin (Nelsons) (just in case the offerer tried to get an uppity attitude about His meat offering.) Just like us today. So you see, offerings then and now, have always been a sacrifice!

Nevertheless, sacrifices did and can become routine. I wonder if that is why the priest had to inspect the offerings themselves before offering them. That prevented man from running out into the yard at the last minute and grabbing anything they had. Just like some of us do not look in our wallet until its time to make the offering. We should be so ready to give that we separate our gift from the rest of the money the day we get our checks cashed. Am I talking to anyone out there?

Of all the sacrifices we make individually, it still can become routine. At one point I was working full time and going to church Monday, Wednesday and Friday nights and Saturday and Sunday mornings. Between house, husband, work and church, I eventually worked out a routine of cooking, cleaning and doing things for myself that was rarely ever ruffled. I enjoyed it and was compelled to go to the services as often as I did but even that became routine. Routine leads to boredom, complacency, sense of duty and sense of thinking we are doing it ourselves. That is why we need to add some salt to whatever we do for Christ.

The salt makes us work. For example, you go to church every Sunday at 11 (routine/sacrifice). Get there at 9 in time for Sunday school (salt). Maybe you already go at 9 for Sunday school (routine/sacrifice). Become a teacher, assistant teacher, or get there early with the superintendent so you can pray and relax, sit quietly in God's presence before class begins or help clean (salt). Salt, then and now literally and spiritually was/is hard to come by. Things that are hard to come by are usually not the things we brag about because we are so far out of our comfort zone that we just want to praise God that we finally accomplished the task.

If we are able to boast, then it is not salt because we have not worked the flesh out. It is just a sacrifice. Now, go put some salt on it! How? Add some preparation to your sacrifice that is so out of your comfort zone that you sweat over it. Hey, isn't sweat salty? Have you ever heard the ancients say, "If you did not sweat, you did not do anything?"

We are supposed to be lively stones, not whiny stones. I am writing this to encourage you. **MOOOOOOOOOVE! GET UP! GOOOOOOOOOOO!** We are the salt of the earth. Our offering must be accompanied by salt. He wanted the offering **seasoned** with salt. Also, God did not ask for a certain amount of salt. But, he did expect the offering to be seasoned enough to be noticed. You can add salt to potatoes to the point where they are too salty (You know some folk that are "Jesus, Jesus, Jesus" all the time and get on everyone's nerves. You know they have a special relationship with God that God tells them everything! And all they do is float in God 24 hours a day and never do anything wrong!). Yet, you can add salt to potatoes to where they are not salted enough, yet you realized that they **have been** salted. Then you can add salt to the point where **everyone** says its just right.

# CHAPTER THREE

*L*et's look closer at some areas of sacrifice and how salt can be added. Then we will do some more discussion on salt in the Old Testament.

The key is that salt, once added, cannot be seen but can be tasted. Sunday morning, you go to morning worship and that is all. It is convenient, routine, already worked into your schedule. Yet it is a sacrifice because anyone would rather lounge around on their day off.

Sacrifices in the Old Testament, although bothersome, were somewhat routine. They knew when to make most sacrifices. It was not a surprise. That is why God wanted something extra. Something that took some effort. Something that was not routine. They were required to add salt every time, but it still was extra work because it was hard to come by (all the time). It had to be searched for and was so precious that one was not obliged to share it for fear of not having enough for themselves. It may have been saved up for and protected. Sacrifices were either already out in the yard, always for sale at the market or a staple always in the cabinet, as it is with our sacrifices. We already know when we are going to church, how long we will be there, what will be required of us, what the ushers have to wear and who is going to preach and for how long. Routine. Salt is the change and is needed to break down the flesh because we do not like change. Change causes us to lose our place sometimes and not know where we are supposed to "be". That is a good thing because it draws us nearer to God in trying to find our new place.

In the Old Testament, it appears that salt had to be searched for. It cost time, money, bargaining, sweat and a decent possibility of not being able to acquire it. Sacrifices could be bragged about. You know there was probably a little bit of "Joe, come look at this fine bull I raised for the sacrifice. I only fed it corn and did not allow it to roam with the other stock." "Martha, look at this fine flour Mr. Abraham saved for me at the market. He said his cousin used extra care to make sure it was suitable for sacrifice, and he gave it all to me." Perhaps, by the time someone found salt, they were so close to being worn out and feeling like they would not get any, that they humbly (not pridefully) put their salt with their sacrifice. Even those who had extra salt may not have bragged about their precious gift for fear they would have to share it.

An example of salt: you know how you felt the last time you prepared a dish for the church dinner. You wondered if you bought enough green beans. You boiled them just right and seasoned them 5 times adding onions, sugar and meat. You got up early to put them in the right dish and into the car and into the church fridge. They needed so much help serving dinner that no one had time to discuss who did what. By the time you finished the day and got out of those shoes (!), you did not care if they liked your beans or not. You were just glad you did your part because you realized that you were not doing it because the pastor or church mother asked you. You were doing it because it pleased God. Often, just volunteering to cook the green beans is adding salt to the sacrifice. Whatever takes us out of our routine is salt.

Okay, so you tried going to Sunday school as well as worship service. Yes, it was pressing to get up earlier and get the children's clothes and attitude (including yours) ready on time. Then you had to sit in a small classroom where you could not hide if you wanted to, exposed to looks, feelings and your own level of knowledge as compared to the other students. Felt kind of sticky, didn't you? Well, my dear, that was the salt. It was not routine, like worship service where it is easy to arrive whenever you feel like it and hide amongst the much larger crowd. No one notices you are daydreaming so you really do not even need to pay attention to the service, much less apply any of it to your life. The salt of going to Sunday school made you sweat, maybe literally, trying to get there on time and preparing your mind to be there all day. You were put on the spot because the teacher could SEE you and ask you a question. And worst, excuse me – I mean best of all, it made you, Mr. Macho and Ms. Self-sufficient, seem like you just might love and need JESUS!

When we apply our salt correctly, by the end of the day, we feel good. We accomplished something that we did not think was possible. We survived the experience and actually enjoyed it. SALT!

For those who pressed your way one time and had the nerve to say "Is this all I came for?" Well, what did you expect? Did you expect the church to have a spectacular service and Sunday school just because you decided to attend both? Honey, they did the same thing they have been doing. Why would you think it would be spectacular because you decided to press your way and go? Those services are no more spectacular than the others. Your attendance is not special or to be celebrated. Your attendance is for your benefit. If you are one of those with the above mentioned attitude, then you did not apply enough salt because the flesh still showed up.

So, you already go to morning worship and Sunday school. You are proud of yourself. Now, guess what God calls it? Sacrifice. It is part of your routine. Now, He wants some salt. In the Old Testament, people found salt in different places. So it is now in the church.

Sunday School may be one man's sacrifice, but another man's salt. If it is your sacrifice, then where is your salt? Go to 8am service. You can take a nap when you get home. Try going to 6pm service. Drop the excuse about needing Sunday evening to spend more time with the family. Check your motivation for this "family time". Some people actually plan Sunday evening outings with their families just so they can tell the pastor that is the reason they cannot make it back to evening service. Admit it. Those outings probably end up more frustrating than fun because your motivation was wrong.  Gotcha!  You end up more frustrated trying to avoid the service than if you would just take the family to church and enjoy the relaxed, spiritual atmosphere of a Sunday evening service.

Why not add mid-week Bible Study as your salt.  Your salt, sister, may be feeding the kids frozen meals or cutting back on your personal expenses so you can buy them dinner and rush out that door to Wednesday night bible study.  Your salt, brother, may be avoiding that chair after dinner and sticking the dishes in the dishwasher and watching the kids while your wife spruces up so all of you can get to  Bible study.  Your salt maybe refusing to be ashamed to tell your male friends that you go to Bible study and do what you can to help your family get there.  You can even bring the food home every Wednesday night or suggest meeting the family at a restaurant so you can leave there and go on to church.  You might even just skip dinner.  Do not tell me you have never made your family hold off two more hours for a meal because you had something else you wanted to do and one more store you wanted to look in or 100 more miles you wanted to drive before stopping.

Some of you attend churches that serve dinner on Wednesday evening for those who do not have time to feed the family at home before Bible Study begins.  Your salt may actually be that you have to eat (for heaven's sake) **church** people's cooking in front of (Oh dear God) church people!  You will actually have to chat and smile with other members of the church after a long day WHEN YOU DO NOT FEEL like being chatty and smiley.  Salt may be actually wearing something "appropriate" all day long at work, so you can go straight to Bible Study after work without the need to rush home to change. You eliminate the excuse that "I went home to change for service and sat down and fell asleep."

**IF** your schedule is sincerely too tight to attend more than one service during the week, maybe you can just go to that one service and actually **do** something auxiliary-wise after you get there. That participation can be your salt. It will make you "taste" better. You will have more of a glow because we do "feel more like running when we do God's will". You will even have the qualifications (living water) to counsel someone else on how to add salt to their sacrifice, since you have successfully done it. Yes. You.

We may all find our salt in different places, but that does not stop us from sharing where we found it. If the children of Israel were like we are, they probably shared information about where salt could be found. So can we. When we find a hard-to-find item or a bargain, we usually share the information. When a choir member asks you to join the choir, she is just trying to help you find some salt.

For those of you who already attend two or three weekly services and joined an auxiliary may think you do not need to add salt. Maybe. Maybe not. If you honestly know that some of that is your salt, then okay. But if all that has become routine because you have been doing it so long, then it is not salt. Been there. Done that. You know, giving a certain amount hurt at one time (salt). Now it does not because you got a raise so you just added it to your tithes but did not increase your offering. Now you need to add what would become salt again.

Your salt could be getting there early to show some dependability and punctuality and offer to be a part of the "meat" of the services. Be so punctual that you cannot hide if you tried. Go that extra mile and participate in an auxiliary that requires you to do something on an "off" day (Tuesday, Thursday, Saturday) like rehearsal, cleaning up, picking up the pastor's robe from the dry cleaners, meeting repairmen, visiting the sick and shut-in. Most of us do not have much more to do for our spouse or children than the others in the church that have a spouse or children and they still manage to add salt. They want to be there and have made a commitment to God to get there.

Organize, especially on church days. A desire to attend church services helps us organize our life in a way that will facilitate us getting there.

It is amazing how we get so frustrated with the thought of chores when the pastor calls revival. We begin to say "I need to wash my windows and I was going to do it that week." Then you skip revival and do the same thing you have been doing all year – watching TV all evening to avoid washing those windows. Get a schedule and put yourself on it!

Consider, the deacon. He does not just come to church for service. On the weekends, he is busy making sure the air or heat is working and checking the restrooms to make sure everything is operating properly. While others are in the barbershop or beauty salon on Friday night or Saturday morning, the deacons are at the church waiting for the plumber or doing the plumbing themselves so the rest of us get to sit back and enjoy the service. The LORD needs, people, like you, to participate in the handling of the little things.

Consider the Sunday School teacher. I have had very few lunches to myself. Most of my lunches have been spent studying Sunday School lessons as a student and a teacher. In one city I spent my lunch hour at the church in noonday prayer service. As the Adult Sunday school teacher/mid-week youth teacher/baptism coordinator/outreach coordinator/minister/student/wife/mentor/business owner/sheep, I have salted my sacrifices. I have used lunch breaks to study for Sunday School, office breaks to make phone calls, nights, weekends and early mornings to study to teach and for myself to pray about myself and my responsibilities and remember that I am still a sheep, too with someone looking over my shoulder. My husband and I have used vacations to go on mission trips. It was all worth it. I have become like David. I am not afraid of a giant because I have been out in the fields fighting lions and bears while others were at home whining and complaining.

While others are out pridefully strutting around, the deacons, ushers, choir members, intercessory prayer warriors, church mothers and the like are in meetings, prayer services, practice or seminars working to prepare themselves and the house of worship so you can be comfortable in the upcoming services. And you have the nerve to say that choir did not sing worth a flip? Are you a provider and a partaker or just a partaker? Are you like the wise virgins and bring "oil" into the house or are you like the foolish virgins and enter the house empty expecting to borrow the "oil" of others? " Haven't you taken long enough? If you have been there at least six months, you have. It is time for you to get up and work so other newcomers can take for a while until it is time for them to get up. "...with all thine offerings thou shalt offer salt."

Think about it. Sacrifice and salt. You just said, "I do not want to put my family through that." That is not what the scriptures said you are supposed to say. Is it really your family you do not want to put through that or is it just an excuse. How you do not want to "put your family through" serving God? We show them examples of bad things like spending too much money in the mall or too much time watching curse-filled movies, but when it comes to serving God we do not want to put them through going to church too much. We put up with wrongdoing and fuss about rightdoing.

You know your family needs Jesus. That is why you are always complaining about how that spouse acts and how those children are hardheaded. I guarantee that when your children become teenagers and late twenties and you "cannot do anything with them", you are going to call on the deacons, pastor or youth officials to admonish them to attend services. Yet, when they are nine, you did not want to "put them through that" going to church so much – 2 days a week for service and one day a week for auxiliary participation. We will keep them involved in 3 or 4 sports activities at a time to keep them busy so they will not get into trouble, but it never occurs to us to drop one sport for a weekly church service that will also keep them out of trouble.

Get over what you did not get to do. Some parents allow their children to do some things because they are still mad at their own parents for not allowing them to do whatever they wanted to do. You give your children too much freedom to show that you can do anything you want to and let your children do the same. The children pay for it by being undisciplined in different areas of their life and that no one including you wants to deal with them.

Parents/leaders, stop raising your children out of spite towards your own parents/leaders. Choose activities and actions because they are healthy or not wrong, not because you want to be the <u>opposite</u> of whoever raised or ruled over you. That is a spirit of rebellion that is passed on to your children and affects bigger areas in their life that they end up not being able to handle very well. Rebellion blocks the advancement of maturity. If you cannot see that some of the things your parents kept you from doing were for your own good and that you should be benefiting from that discipline right now, then you are not a mature person. You are still a pouty, immature, rebellious child yourself and that is what you are going to raise. See Proverbs 12:15, 15:5, 17:10, **17:21 and 18:2.

In the Old Testament, children knew the purpose of all the labor of sacrifices and finding salt. Deuteronomy 6:4-7 "Hear, o Israel: the Lord our God is one Lord: and thou shalt love the Lord thy God with all thine heart, and with all thy soul, and with all thy might."

And these words, which I command thee this day, shall be in thine heart:

**"And thou shalt teach them diligently unto thy chil-**

**dren and shalt talk of them when thou sittest in thine house, and when thou walkest by the way, and when thou liest down, and when thou risest up."**

Always saying "I'm not going to that service." I don't have time for all this church" or sitting on the phone all day long talking about people in front of your children is not what God meant! Yeah, you are diligently teaching, but that is not what is supposed to be taught. Children learn to be hypocrites from adults. They learn how to turn off their spirituality during the week and turn it back on during Sunday service. They learn to act one way at home and put on a show at church. I have taught children. They see and they talk about what they see.

Have you ever complained about other people and their children always being in the spotlight? It is because they are there! The parents and the children. They show up regularly enough to be depended upon. Again, I hear what some of you are saying. The true church is not a building, it is in the people in the building. Well, when you decided to get right with the Lord, you headed for a church. It was good enough to get you started, so why is it so trivial now? If you are so against this notion of a physical church building, then have you really been changed into a new creature or are you feeling guilty so you strike back? You are probably not out laboring in the hedges and highways, either. If this is striking a nerve, do not strike back. Strike out heading for your church leader to sign up for a job to do in the service of the Lord (smile).

The lack of salt with our sacrifice will cause us to walk into the church with an "I'm doing everyone a favor by being here" attitude. So we end up walking out having not received a thing from the Lord because we were not open to receiving. Why do we think anybody needs to see us to be happy? The one who has added salt walks into the same sanctuary with the humility of appreciation for the effort it takes to keep it going and a heart full of praise because God allowed him to serve and blessed him with the time to shop for, learn about and complete the problem solving work needed to make sure his part was completed successfully. That deacon, usher, choir member, praise team member, mother is thanking God for grace and mercy in blessing them to complete their tasks, whether it was finding the right uniform, getting the sound system fixed or learning the new song.

Ladies, let's go back to that example of preparing dinner for Sunday worship. Your whole schedule changes but at the end of Sunday you feel great about the service and your accomplishments because you accepted a challenge and succeeded. Rather than going home after work on Thursday, you had to rush to the grocery store to buy food to prepare. Instead of getting your hair done on a leisurely Saturday, you had to rush in to the shop after work on Friday evening and stay late to get it done because on Saturday you would be cooking for Sunday. On Sunday morning instead of lounging around until ten, you had to get up early to finish the peas and fried chicken, make five trips to load the car instead of one **and** you had to get to service early so you could unload your car. You begin feeling frustrated, but once you get there and sit down you feel great about your accomplishments so you praise the Lord! Any other time you would just drag into church like it was a chore.

We are to flavor like salt. Remember earlier, I reminded you that salt, once applied, cannot be seen but can be "tasted." People can tell when salt has been added. Real work makes us humble and humility makes us seasoned and better tasting. Our salt is not supposed to be seen with the naked eye. We are not supposed to brag about what we went through to get to service. If there is bragging, then there is no humility. If there is no humility, then there is no work. If there is no work, then there is no salt. It is not visible, but the results of its use are there. God wants us to "flavor" the earth. Just like He wanted the children of Israel to flavor their sacrifices.

How does that apply to us? Gathering the salt, taking extra time, money, effort to do something extra, kills the flesh which makes us noticeably different and better. When we do extra for the Lord, no one sees what we go through and how it affects our life. No one but us and God sees how it affects our family's schedule, budget and way of thinking. But the congregation sees how it affects our attitude, blessings and level of maturity. They may not know why we are different, but they see the results.

If you already attend church regularly (sacrifice) and decide to become an usher (salt), that uniform (salt) means denying the fleshly desire to be a fashion plate. You become more compassionate and less self-centered and it shows even when he is not scheduled to usher. That little bit of salt brought out the better person in you and it shows. Your salt is there. Others can taste it. It is written all over you.

Once I was approached by a man who accused me of being one of those holy people. I admitted it and asked him how did he know. He indignantly said, "It is written all over you!" In the blink of an eye, the Lord gave me a reply. I said "Well, its supposed to be according to Matthew 5:13!" Using the example of a woman preparing food for Sunday dinner or a man doing his deacon duties seems rather trivial, but that is where most church members live. Most are not preachers who are up before the congregation every time the church doors open. Even ministers and shepherds are required to add salt. No one is so high that they are exempt from obeying God's word.

Get out that shaker and start applying salt to your sacrifice. Most of the people in the church never or rarely ever walk past the third row, unless they are going to put their money in the offering pan. Finding salt takes some effort. If it does not require effort, it is not salt. "If <u>we</u> do it in our own strength, it is not salt. If we chose to add where it is <u>convenient</u>, it is not salt. Salt is doing that thing that is so far from our comfort zone that we dare not brag about it because we really do not want to do it anyway. Everything looks just fine without our input. Yeah, it does, but we do not "taste" right. Now, let's use the scriptures to elaborate more on the benefits of adding salt to your sacrifice.

# CHAPTER FOUR

*It was used to heal the bitter waters*

**II** Kings 2:20-22 "And he said, bring me a new cruse, and put salt therein. And they brought it to him. And he went forth unto the spring of the waters, and cast the salt in there, and said, Thus saith the Lord, I have healed these waters; there shall not be from thence anymore death or barren land. So the waters were healed unto this day, according to the saying of Elisha which he spake."

Salt will heal your bitter water. John 7:37, 38 says "In the last day, that great day of the feast, Jesus stood and cried, saying, if any man thirst, let him come unto me and drink. He that believeth on me, as the scripture hath said, out of his belly shall flow rivers of <u>living</u> water."

All people thirst. All people drink. Dare I say that all of us have "water" in our belly. Which might suggest that all water is not living because all do not "come unto Jesus" to drink.  The water in II Kings 2 was used for drinking and watering crops.   When the waters were healed, they no longer caused physical death to those who drank it nor barrenness to the land.

How does this apply to us?    Salt will heal our bitter water that lie in our belly.  If we make an extra effort to participate, i.e. put some salt with our sacrifice, that salt will make us "taste" better.  We will come in the sanctuary happier – not bitter, angry, looking for everything to be wrong, frustrated and complaining.

Salt can be as simple as admitting that there are some people in church that can do something as good as you can.  A busy person has little time to cause irritation in the church because they are busy trying to get **their** part done.  If we are busy rowing our own boat, we do not have time to have our nose stuck over in John's boat trying to see how he is rowing.  Our job (salt) will bring living water in the form of positive conversation and encouragement to others.

Example:  a sacrifice is a dead cow.  A sacrifice with salt is a steak with some flavor.  We are the dead cow because we died to the fleshly desire that wants to sit back and do nothing.  We become the steak with flavor when we add salt by doing something extra. When people see us without salt, they make that same face we make when we eat something that has no natural salt.  The water that comes out of our belly does not edify.  People will say, "Don't go his way. He looks mad."  Just as we do today when we advise someone to avoid the potatoes because they do not have any salt on them.

Without salt, we vomit our bitter water onto others

accusing everyone else of being the problem. More than once I have been accused of not taking the time to speak to someone before Sunday morning worship started. You know those kind of people who do not want to look at their own life so they spend much of their time picking on other people's lives. So many times I have just wanted to go off on these type of people, but the Lord reminds me that if they had salt on their own sacrifice, they would not even notice what I am or am not doing. They have chosen to avoid adding salt to their sacrifice (knowingly or unknowingly), therefore they have much time to observe but with the wrong attitude. If they understood the whole picture and was less self-centered, they would see that I arrived at church at 9:30 or 10am while they did not get there until 10 or 11:30. They would see that I stood on my feet for 45 minutes teaching the adult Sunday school class and by the time they walked in at 11:30 or 12, I had spoken to or helped several people. When Mr. or Ms. "You-act like-you-don't-have-time-to-pay-attention-to-me" was just coming in, I could have been slightly tired of standing and talking while teaching the class, I just wanted to sit down and con-template the beginning of the service. I probably did miss speaking to them somewhere in all those things I had just done and all the other things I still needed to do (depending on what Sunday it was) like ministerial intercessory prayer, quick prayer about altar counseling duties, overseeing the youth preparedness for the program if it was Youth Sunday, preparing the baptism candidates if it was Baptism Sunday. You know, gathering all my salt together and putting it on my sacrifice. The bitter waters of "she did not speak to me" would have been made sweeter if that person had only added salt by getting up earlier and helping me do some of those things.

We have to listen to rivers of unsalted, bitter waters – complaints, "the service isn't right", "they took too long", "why do we have to come back again tonight?" The usual. Bitter water kills. Living water gives life. Enough said? People, eventually others either die from your bitter waters or stop using (listening to) your bitter waters like the people of Jericho stopped using those bitter waters.

We can try to salt others if we can find a "salt shaker". We can suggest areas to find salt, but we cannot put it on them. Some of us do desperately try to find salt for others so they will stop bugging us. But, each one of us must choose to add salt. We can encourage each other to join the usher board, the sick and shut-in committee, the teaching staff, or the get-there-on-time club, but we cannot make it happen. Salt avoiders, stop envying salt adders and try to be like us! Stop acting like a Philistine trying to kill Samson and just try asking Samson how can you get the same strength he has!!! When you salt your sacrifice, your bitter water will be healed. No more bitter, nasty comments, rolling eyes and misjudgments.

Some people complain about things they supposedly cannot put up with in Sunday School or evening worship service, but they manage to handle those same things when they go to the mall or at work. The kids are too bad to take to church, but you can carry them to the mall. The hair spray, carpet dust, perfume, powered-scented baby wipes or deodorant give you an allergic rash when you encounter them at church, but you can handle all those elements at work, in restaurants, on the bus, at the beauty salon or in the grocery store. Your ears can handle the noisy television at home, or the machines or phones ringing at work all day long, but the drums at church are just too loud. Stop lying! Bitter water. When you add some salt to your sacrifice, your bitter water will become rivers of living water flowing from your belly. Your "cannots" will become "cans" as in "I can do all things through Christ Jesus who strengthens me!" Behold old things ( I can't) have passed away and all things (I can!!!) have become new!!!"

# CHAPTER FIVE

## Salt as a Purifier

According to the New World Dictionary, a purifier rids of pollution, frees from guilt, sin, or incorrect or corrupting elements. We tend to take God's work and act like it was our idea. We fix it up a little bit because what He said to do just does not sound quite good enough. Purify means to free from incorrect or corrupting elements. Adding a little salt to our sacrifice will purify the work. It will remove our ideas so only God's will be left.

Remember earlier we discussed those who are excited only when they participate in the program. A maturing, faith-walking Christian understands that all things work together for the good of them that love God, to them who are the called according to His purpose (Romans 8:28).

Some saints sit with arms folded until it is time for them to testify or speak or sing. They complain about every part

of the service except their part. They talk about how great
the service is only when they play a part in it, otherwise,
they have nothing good to say. When they get up to do their
part, they are so excited you can hardly keep up with them.
They want everyone else to holler and scream for them like
they are the show. Man tries to take credit for God's ideas.
Plus for those who are of the attitude of "get with me, but
I'm not gonna' get with you" are very critical and think
everyone else will be just as critical of them. Example: I
turn my nose up at everyone's singing. So when I get up to
sing, I automatically think everyone will turn their nose up
at me. Sooooo, I automatically get angry at everyone.

Arrogant, prideful people are never satisfied with the
amount of attention they get and hate it when anyone else in
the world gets any kind of attention. Isn't it unmannerly to
only be excited when you are on the program? Isn't it
unmannerly to go to church only when you have a testimo-
ny then try to stay up for 30 minutes? Isn't it unmannerly
when you insists that you are the only one qualified to lead,
usher, witness, sing because God gave you the only gift in
the world?

Salt was used in the belief that it purified new babies.
One problem with the work we do in our churches is motivation. Why are we doing what we are doing? Yes, what
we are doing is good, but why are we doing it?

I Corinthians 3:9-15, 18-21, "According to the grace of
God which is given unto me, as a wise master builder, I
have laid the foundation, and another buildeth thereon. But
let **every man take heed how he buildeth thereupon**. For
other foundation can no man lay than that is laid, which is

Jesus Christ."

When we begin a specific project for the Lord, the foundation (idea) is His and we must be careful not to build our own little "I did this all by myself" walls and roof on top of it? Shame on you. God gives us a foundation of spiritual gifts and callings and He wants us to attend and participate in the service on His terms.

"Now if any man build upon this foundation gold, silver, precious stones, wood, hay, stubble; **Every man's work shall be made manifest; for the day shall declare it, because it shall be revealed by fire; and the fire shall try every man's work of what <u>sort</u> it is.**"

"If any man's work abide which he hath built thereupon, he shall receive a reward. If any man's work shall be burned, he shall suffer loss; but he himself shall be saved; yet so as by fire." (I Corinthians 3:13-15)

When we start wrong, we will end up all wrong. We know when we have started with the wrong intentions. Salt will purify that. How? Our sacrifices have become so routine that we have come to believe the church needs us. Gal 4:8,9, "Howbeit then, when ye knew not God, ye did service unto them which by nature are no Gods. But now, after that ye have known God, or rather are known of God, how turn ye gain to the weak and beggarly elements, whereunto ye **desire** again to be in bondage?" Our flesh was weak and beggarly. That is why we felt the need to receive Christ. Now, we think our flesh is doing everything instead of God.

We have come to believe that we plan the church program and God carries it out rather than the other way around. We believe we choose the plan of salvation and

God agrees with whatsoever we desire. Philippians 2:12, 13 reads "...work out your own salvation with fear and trembling. For it is God which worketh in you both the will and to do of **His** good pleasure." In <u>My Utmost for His Highest</u>, Oswald Chamber's gift of words of wisdom interprets that as meaning we are to **work** out of us our **own idea** of **salvation,** and allow God to work in us His will. I tend to believe Chamber's wisdom rather than those who believe the scripture means that God has special salvation for some people who are allowed to forego His yoke, remain in bondage to live as they please and continue to share the name of God with everyone else. And it is bondage. Whenever we are afraid to do what is right because we do not want everyone looking at us or we do not want to fit outside the crowd or we have been threatened, that is bondage. Salvation's purpose is to bring **liberty** to do what is right and temperate, no matter who is looking. We must decrease our idea of how salvation ought to be so that God's idea of salvation can increase in us.

What is our MOTIVATION? Salt will purify. Yeah, we sacrifice, attend church services and maybe even go to prayer meeting and sing in the choir. When those activities have become routine, our motivation is in jeopardy and we need to add some salt. We get so complacent that the devil slips in and says the auxiliary cannot make it without us. We become blind to the fact that churches, choirs, usher boards, deacon boards and pastors have succeeded for years before we were even thought of but we think they can do nothing right without us! That attitude calls for salt.

We need to chose an activity we do not particularly like.

Some faith work we do not think we are capable of doing. That is salt. It will purify our motives. By the time we find that salt (preparing for that job we had to really call on God to know how to do) we are so close to feeling like we may fail that we do not care what other people think. We will just want to make it to the altar and present **our** salt, i.e. succeed for God.

Our salt can be in the form of foregoing those things church used to be about. New outfit, new tie, fresh eye catching hairdo, new nail job, new shoes, "I'm righteous" attitude. Let go of the vanity of it all. You men who think it's "punk" to go to church with a hair cut may find your salt in cutting your hair and looking clean for a minute. If you are one of those types who are always doing the opposite, not because its what you want to or are supposed to do but because it is the opposite of everyone else. Your salt could be conforming to the image, which basically boils down to obedience.

Another example: everyone is asked to wear yellow and you are aware of it, but you decide to be an individual and wear orange. Your salt needs to be obedience. Forget self and obey. Salt purifies your motives. It takes all the air of pride out so the glory of God can show.

We have become so mundane and so entranced with our routines of going to church at certain times, on certain occasions, sitting in the same place and singing the same songs. Our sacrifices are barely sacrifices and do not mean much of anything to us anymore. They do not cause a change in us. In the Old Testament, the sacrifices were always the same, but the salt was what made them pay attention. Each

time of offering, the procurement of salt may never have
been the same. Remember, it was so precious it was used
to pay soldiers. The search, acquisition, price and amount
may not have always been the same. There probably was
no comfort zone when it came to finding the salt for the sacrifice. The salt does take us out of our comfort zone.

Without salt, we forget all of the faith and work is for
our benefit. God is already in Heaven. We begin to believe
that we are doing Him favor. We show off to our friends
and neighbors when they see our service for the Lord
instead of remembering that He is the master and we are the
clay trying to be shaped into His image. Galatians 3:3 says,
"Are ye so foolish having begun in the spirit are ye now
made perfect by the flesh?"

When we give up something we want to give there is
always pride there because the flesh is going to be pleased.
When we give up something we do not want to give, the
pride is GONE. When we give up extra time, money, space
in our car for a rider to go to church, extra effort to be in the
choir or be part of a committee, our pride is gone because
we need to call on Jesus for help. By the time we are finished we have no desire to brag because we are just grate-
ful God got us through it so we would not look like a failure. The salt purifies the  motive.

# CHAPTER SIX

*Salt Kills*

(Romans 8:13 and Colossians 3:5)

*J*udges 9:45 – "And Abilmelech fought against the city all that day; and he took the city, and slew the people that was therein, and beat down the city and sowed it with salt." Abilmelech poured salt over the land he conquered so that nothing else would grow out of it. He wanted to show that he fully conquered it.

We first kill the flesh which is the sacrifice. We kill it by getting out of the bed, leaving the TV alone and going to go to church. Then we make sure it stays dead by going that extra mile. Perhaps by getting to church on time or early. The salt of arriving early is that we put ourselves in the position to be asked to participate (open up the devotion or say the opening prayer or read the opening scripture, watch over the nursery, etc). When we get there early, we are visible which can be a difficult position in the church.

When we make ourselves visible, the assumption is that we are also available.  The pastor may even come and speak to you and get close enough to see in your eyes or something silly like that. Honey, when the spirit gets ready to uncover, you do not have to be in close proximity of the person to see it.

Condemnation or conviction comes from inside a person not from outside.  That is why alot of people try to hide in church.  They already feel bad about their life because they know better.

When we are visible, we may be asked to do something. Salt helps us die to self and learn to say yes when God has already told us that we have not been doing enough.  Our flaws are more visible.  We are  criticized more. We learn to deal with it, fix the problem or tell people to get over it if It is just their own little personal problem.  We learn to give God the glory.  All of it is uncomfortable.

Salt kills all that flesh that does not want to be asked to do anything. Salt kills the flesh so that rejection, criticism, failure, praise, and the like will not affect us in a bad way. We eventually learn to go to church and participate with pure motives which include  worshipping and praising our Maker.

# CHAPTER SEVEN

## Salt Breaks Down/Decomposes

Luke 14:35 reads, "Salt is good: but if the salt have lost his savour, wherewith shall it be seasoned? It is neither fit for the land, nor yet for the dunghill; but men cast it out. He who hath ears to hear, let him hear."

Salt is used in reference to the dunghill. It was put on dung to help it break down faster so that it could be used as fertilizer. Salt with our sacrifice will break down all parts of our thoughts, knowledge, spirit and motives and will leave the good parts of those areas that God can use.

We go to church, but sometimes we stink! We think we are somebody all by ourselves and do not need Christ. When dung is broken down, it does not stink anymore or as bad. One may go to church and sing lead or preach but it stinks to God because it is done out of envy, strife or malice towards others in the church. Someone may be doing a good job on the mother board but only to prevent someone else from getting the job.

Salt purifies remember? Salt breaks down all that stinky stuff put in our mind, spirit, and soul by hurts, rejections, disappointments and anger that causes us to be spiteful, vain, jealous, competitive and afraid to move on in what Christ wants to do in your life. Salt will cause us to begin doing things according to Christ's plans and our sacrifices do not stink in His nostrils.

When we operate in our calling, people are edified, grow, and bring forth fruit just like decomposed dung does when it is used to fertilize the planting ground. Salt breaks down that dung of bitterness, anger, strife, heresies, envy – stuff that the body cannot use – and brings out peace, love, meekness, temperance, gentleness, and goodness. The mother that is running things out of envy to keep someone else from running them, begins to do that same work out of goodness or gives the job to its rightful owner. That preacher who is preaching out of bitterness to beat someone else or because the deacons will not pay him much will begin to preach out of the spirit of love. The singer trying to sing better than someone else out of envy will begin to sing those same songs out of joy and gentleness. We play instruments, lead songs, teach, preach, usher, and deacon for all kinds of wrong reasons and bad spirits. There is a difference in the person who no longer does things for evil reason. We notice even if we do not understand. The salt may not be seen, but it can be tasted! The salt makes the dung good for fertilizing. The salt breaks down that flesh that is warring against the spirit. It moves it/decomposes it out so the spirit of God can come forth and operate.

Sacrifices become routine.  That is why you sacrifice to attend church, but you can easily complain about the whole service without conviction.  Put some salt with that sacrifice.  The results will be the good left in you that God will use to fertilize seeds in others.

Galatians 5:22-26, "But the fruit of the Spirit is love, joy,  peace, longsuffering, gentleness, goodness, faith, meekness, temperance:  against such there is no law.  And they that are Christ's have crucified the flesh with the affections and lusts.  If we live in the spirit, let us also walk in the spirit.  Let us not be desirous of vain glory, provoking one another, envying one another."

So you want to know where  you can find some salt.  Seek God.  Observe others in the services.  Talk to those who are in auxiliaries that seem to interest you.  Ask for the good, the bad and the ugly.  Definitely talk to your pastor.  Pray about it for a little while - not for years, now.  Then get some Holy Ghost boldness and join in.

Get up.  Get going.   When that  becomes routine, add some more salt.

# CONCLUSION

*Places to look for Salt.*

*I*f You do not attend service, start going.

If you are already going to Sunday morning worship, go to Sunday School.

If you already go to Sunday School and Morning Worship, offer to teach a class and be honest about how often you are willing to do it.

Note: Pray that your church is sheep-oriented. Jesus compared people to sheep and overseers to shepherds. He was not/is not controlling or demanding. If you research sheep and shepherds, you will see that sheep did not cater to the shepherds and treat them like fine china. The shepherds looked out for the sheep. Read Ezekiel. Hopefully, you attend a church that has disciple-oriented leadership that will not condemn a sheep to hell for saying "I don't know how to do that. Will you help me?" Hopefully, you attend a church where the leaders have enough compassion to not totally dismiss a sheep when they say "I can do this once/twice a week/month because I have other obligations/not enough confidence at this point to obligate myself more/I want to be able to sit and learn more myself.")

So, you already go to Sunday School, Morning Worship and arrive on time. Go to weekly Bible Study as often as you truly can.

## Join an auxiliary.

If you already joined an auxiliary, seek a leadership role in that auxiliary.

If you go to service late, begin arriving on time. If you are always late because you have issues with church and its people or you need to make an entrance, pray to get over your issues. Dare to be healed.

If you are late because you have to eat, skip the meal. Eat later. If you have an illness that requires you to eat at certain times, don't beat me up. I'm not talking to you.)

If you are insecure about your looks and just have to have a new hairdo, clothes, nails, suits, shoes, car wash, haircut every week, dare to love yourself just the way you are and really face your insecurity/arrogance (whatever it truly is) and just for once, believe that not everyone is looking at you. Dare to be healed.

If you are so insecure that you spend time putting someone else down to make yourself look good, try admitting that you are insecure and realize that your criticisms hinder you from worshipping in spirit and in truth. Your salt may be allowing yourself to be healed so you can leave other folk alone!!!!! **Dare to be healed.**

Stop hiding behind sarcasm, the microphone, your songs and testimonies. Add some salt by actually doing what the word says and going to talk to that person, one on one. (Matthew 18:15.) Don't be chicken. Repent. Submit to God and your spirit of anger will leave. I do not care what others may be doing to you, your spirit of anger is not justified. Dare to be healed.

Pray through to the point where you can still enjoy service even if no one calls your name. If you get mad because no one called your name, then it is a clear indication that at that particular point you were not thinking about worshipping God in spirit and in truth. You were thinking about your own flesh! If you need to hear it all the time, it is probably because you feel like you are not doing your job well enough and you think you do not deserve the title. When we know who we are, we are not really worried about other people knowing who we are. Dare to be healed.

Join the usher board or choir. The requirement of wearing that uniform or robe twice a month will help smother that "My clothes look better and are more expensive than yours" attitude and you will feel much better and bondage free. It is bondage and exhausting trying to make money and time every week to go shopping for clothes that will make other people's heads turn. Thank God for clergy shirts. They are uncomfortable and nothing to get excited about. They will keep a minister humble.

If you hate a particular area of worship, like Outreach or Shut-in services, participate at least one time. If you already have, participate one more time. Be a big girl or boy and just humble yourself there under the mighty hand of God. One day you needed outreach and one day you will probably need Shut-in services.

If you are afraid to talk, offer to read the announcements or the scripture lesson during Sunday School. Start somewhere.

If you do not know how to get involved, offer to bring a dish to the next fellowship dinner. It will help you meet people who can tell you how to get more involved.

If you are always involved in activities or moving around during the service, dare to shut up, sit down and take a day off during service. I guarantee the church will go on without your input or the leaders will be forced to really seek God for someone else to help instead of always relying on a faithful few. Sometimes leaders are just too lazy to "harvest" their other members. They just do not work hard enough to try to raise others in the church to do something (until after they have worn out or run off the other workers.)

If you think you can do everything better, try giving someone else's idea a try or shutting off that critical voice in your head every time you want to critique others. The world did revolve pretty well by itself before you got here. Even if you can do it better, relax, the world is still revolving anyway! Offer advice if they ask. Shut up if they don't.

If there is someone in the church that you just cannot stand, offer to work with them. Getting to know them may help or confirm your suspicions. Either way, it is all helpful information.

Maybe you are in a church where they will not let you do anything. Go out into the hedges and highways or even another country and lead others to Christ. Who can condemn you for obeying Matthew 28:18-20? It would be strange/double-minded of them to say you can't witness but then they grin in the faces of those you bring into their church through your witnessing.

If you think you are horrible at everything you do, dare to lead a church project and prove yourself wrong or maybe right. At least give it a try. You may find out what is or is not your purpose in God's plan.

If you have a problem with everybody, dare to look inside of yourself and see if/that you are the problem.

If there is someone at church that does not like you, intercede for them that God will bless them to get over you because you desire that they reign in Heaven also. That's love. Note: The spirit of jealousy wants to be <u>like</u> you and is probably satisfied working beside you. The spirit of envy actually wants to <u>be</u> you and will try to destroy you and take your place. It hates you and tries to kill you. Intercede without ceasing!!!! It works! Ask some of my former enemies, **if** you can find them (Psalms 37:1, Psalms 1:4-6, Psalms 23: 5).

If you are still rolling your eyes or having bad thoughts about someone, dare to forgive them or admit your wrongdoing. Drop that grudge for a change and read the one right above this one again.

Whatever makes you uncomfortable, try doing that! Just trying it may be your salt!

## Repent!

Habakkuk 2:2 –"And the Lord answered me, and said, Write the vision, and make it plain upon tables, that he may run that readeth it."

Through the grace of God,

I have written it.

I have made it plain.

You have read it.

Now, RRRRRRRRRUUUUUUUUNNNNNNNNNNN!